Once upon a
DINKELSBÜHL

Once upon a DINKELSBÜHL

Story by Patricia Lee Gauch

Pictures by Tomie de Paola

G. P. Putnam's Sons · New York

Library of Congress Cataloging in Publication Data
Gauch, Patricia Lee. Once Upon a Dinkelsbühl
SUMMARY: A retelling of the German legend in which
the children of medieval Dinkelsbühl confront the leader
of the Swedish soldiers plundering their town.
1. Legends—Germany—Dinkelsbühl (City) 2. Dinkelsbühl, Ger. (City)—History—Juvenile literature. [1. Folk-
lore—Germany. 2. Dinkelsbühl, Germ. (City)—History
—Fiction] I. De Paola, Thomas Anthony. II. Title.
PZ8.1.G16870n   [398.2]   [E]   76-29356
ISBN 0-399-20560-8   ISBN 0-399-61049-9 lib. bdg.

To my mother
who has always believed in children

To begin,
you see there in that soft, soft green meadow the tiny city circled round
by a great gray wall? That is Dinkelsbühl. Pretty little Dinkelsbühl.
But look closer, you see how the flowerboxes are empty? How dull the
doorknobs are? How tight the shutters are shut? And no one is laughing
here.

Three different times,
three different armies with three different flags flying swept over Dinkelsbühl with flashing swords and snorting horses. "Bread! Bread!" they shouted. But they took shoes and clothes and money and men. They smashed doors and battered gates. They broke windows. And the Dinkelsbühlians have not been quite the same since!

There, Mae the baker. She used to bake fifteen rows of gingerbread people a day. Now she stays to herself and bakes only bread.

And the tailor Tim? He could sew a stitch and dance a jig at the same time. Now his door is shut as tight as a lord's and he sews under the stairs.

Even the Bürgermeister who used to give great windy speeches in the marketplace now comes out only now and then to say there is nothing to say.

No, no one is quite the same!

Well, that is not altogether true. Lore, the gatekeeper's daughter, is still exactly Lore. (That is Lore up there, balancing on the tower wall. Behind her? Oh, that is Hans, her cat.)

Lore knows every crooked street and secret cranny in all Dinkelsbühl. (There, now she and Hans are already off the wall, sitting in one of her secret crannies.) Lore hates to see the streets so gray and gloomy. She hates to see Mae and Tim and the Bürgermeister and all the Dinkelsbühlians so so sour and stern.

Sometimes Lore, being exactly Lore, tries to do something about it. She ups and says to Mae, "I shall punch your bread for you, Mae. Then you can make more gingerbread." Or to Tim, "I could spin the thread, dear Tim, if you'd but dance!" And so on and so on. But if her papa catches her, he says, "Lore, Lore, you can change nothing! Don't you know children should be seen and not heard?"

Did you see
all those faces peering in the window behind Hans the cat? Those are
the other children. The freckled boy is Willie. The girl with long
braids, that is Elsa. And there are Fritzie, Eva, Frieda, Jan behind them.
Oh, and Georgie and Paul are standing on the sill. Anyway…they don't
agree with Lore's papa at all.

They think what Lore says is just right. They like what she does too. After chores when Lore says, "Let's pick wild flowers by the moat," they all run to pick wild flowers.

When she says, "Let's climb to the top of the clock tower," they wind behind her like a vine.

When she says, "Let's go swimming in the fountain," they do!

Of course, if the other Dinkelsbühlians catch the children running and chattering through the streets and around the moat, well, they say just what Lore's papa says:
"Shhhhh! Children should be seen and not heard!"

Perhaps down deep the Dinkelsbühlians are thinking, "Shhhh, if we bother no one, perhaps no one will bother us. No greedy kings, no noblemen, no soldiers in tin suits."

And perhaps they are right. Look, as the days pass, the grass grows up between the cobblestones. The vines twist over the walls. But those kings are riding right by. That army didn't even stop. Those noblemen don't bother the city at all!

But, wait,
it is later, a summer night. The towers stand bold in the moonlight, and over the hill, aren't those torches coming this way? And soldiers …pulling cannon!

And now, a colonel with shiny buttons and a giant sword who rides up
to the gate and shouts,
"Meat and bread or your lives in bed!"

The Dinkelsbühlians have heard that before. Soldiers who ask for bread and steal the town! The lights of the city wink on. There is the gatekeeper's light. And there, there is Lore's. Look, Lore is already mad. She remembers the other armies, too. Quickly, she stuffs Hans into her sewing basket. Then she runs to the cupboard and loads her arms with dishes and pans and anything she can throw!

But her papa is angry too and he has other ideas. He puts her in her room and locks the door. "No, Papa. Let me do something!" Lore says. But her papa doesn't listen. "This is no time for children," he says, clicking the key. He runs very quietly to the tower-gate window.

All the Dinkelsbühlians are waiting and watching behind the wall. (They have all hidden the children safely away.)

"Meat and bread or your lives in bed!" the colonel bellows again. His cannoneer is lining up his biggest brass cannon. But as he brings his torch to it, the Dinkelsbühl bell gongs. It is a signal. The Dinkelsbühlians pour down a rain of rocks, pans, wood, and anything small enough to throw.

When she hears the bell, Lore shouts through the keyhole, "Let me out, Papa!" But no one answers. She tries to squeeze through the window, but it is too small. She hammers the lock, but it won't break. "Papa!" she calls again.

But Lore's papa is busy in the tower. The soldiers have lighted their cannon.

BARROOOM!

The cannonball rips through the gate. The horses race through the streets, and now the soldiers are storming into the houses. They are knocking down doors. They are taking bread, meat, shoes, candlesticks —whatever is not nailed to the floor.

Lore's papa, who is not so quick on his feet, just makes it to Lore's room before the soldiers. He hides her behind him, but she pulls away. "Papa," she mutters, "I don't want to hide. I want to do something!" "Lore, Lore, won't you ever learn?" he says, just as a soldier puts his heel through the street door.

He pushes Lore and the gatekeeper with all the other Dinkelsbühlians into the marketplace where they can only watch while their houses are emptied.
Lore is steaming.
There goes her red coat, her shiny kneeboots. Oh, and her blue daisy coverlet. Everything! Almost everything. They have not carried out the round sewing basket. At least Hans is safe.

And, surely, it is almost over.

But wait. The colonel with the silver buttons and the giant sword is steering his horse through the crowd. Behind him three men are carrying bigger, brighter torches.

"Fools, fools, fools," he shouts. "You dare to fight the colonel?" His eyes sweep the faces. "Then I dare to burn your city down!"

The Dinkelsbühlians gasp. Lore's cheeks flush red. Burn Dinkelsbühl? Its wall, its crooked streets and secret crannies, its fountain? Burn Dinkelsbühl? Suddenly Lore remembers the basket still in her room! Burn Hansie, too?

"Papa," she pleads right out loud, "now we must do something."

But the soldiers are already prodding the Dinkelsbühlians toward the city gate like so many sheep. One of the soldiers has her own papa by the arm. It is too late.

The Dinkelsbühlians begin to stream toward...but wait, where is Lore? That girl! Oh, yes, there she is, looking through the tangle of arms and legs at Willie digging in his heels, at Elsa pushing a private back, and at Fritzie biting a sergeant's hand. Now Lore herself ducks into the crowd. No one sees her, but there she is all right, whispering to Georgie, now Peter, Eva, Fritzie, Frieda, Jan and Paul and....

Suddenly it is dark.

All the Dinkelsbühlians are under the tower gate and coming out on the other side. But where have all the children gone? "Lore, Lore!" calls the gatekeeper. "Fritzie!" "Eva!" "Willie!" All the mamas and papas are frantically looking for their children.

Then they see them! The children are running like wild ponies back to the marketplace behind Lore. Oh, those three guards will stop them! No, the children skim their fingertips. They can't escape that angry horseman. But, look, they fool him by running around the fountain. And the wagon. Nothing stops them, nothing until …

they reach the colonel, sitting on his horse. He is like a great giant with his sword and buttons shiny in the torchlight. "Away!" he shouts. "Away!"

But even now Lore, being exactly Lore, stands firm and says, rather softly, rather kindly, "Sir, please listen!"

The colonel whips his horse around; its tail scatters the children. But Lore runs around in front of him again.

"Sir," she says (her voice is not quite so soft or kind), "Could you please listen?"

Still the colonel doesn't listen. "They are like flies! Gnats!" he bellows. "Get them out of here!"

But before the soldiers can move, Fritzie grabs the colonel's boots.
Willie holds on to the saddle. Eva won't let his leg go. The others form
a ring, and Lore stands directly in front of him once more.

The colonel climbs down slowly and glares at Lore.
Lore glares at the colonel.
"You, too, are fighting the colonel!"
"No, sir," she says.
"Yes, miss," he says. (He is growing angry.)
"NO, SIR!" she says. (She is growing angry.)
"NO?" he asks.
His face is only a nose away from Lore's, but suddenly
she can see his eyes listen!
"NO…sir." Quickly she grabs some bread. "You are hungry, take this
bread. Your feet are sore, these shoes will fit. This cloth might patch
your coat. Take it all, sir, but, sir, please, sir, leave us our city, sir."

Do you hear that growing hum?

That is all the children—Willie, Elsa, Fritzie, Eva, Georgie, Paul, Hannah, Frieda, Jan, Peter, Ronald, Charles, Susanne, Julie, Richard, Anna—all of them piling food and clothing at the colonel's feet and saying,

"Please, sir, colonel, don't burn Dinkelsbühl!"

And now, suddenly, the town is so quiet. Shhhhhh. Listen. Even the soldiers on their horses are like statues in a castle courtyard. But the colonel is saying nothing. He is used to people running from him. He is used to people fighting him. But he is not used to…this. He looks at Lore and the other children. He looks from face to face.

Whatever is he going to do?

Hit them?

Shoot them?

Trample them?

Finally he reaches for his sword, waves it in the air, and shouts,

"Put out the torches!"

Put out the torches? The soldiers, Lore, the children, even the Dinkelsbühlians peering in from the city gate cannot believe their ears.

"Put them out now," he bellows again. "Take only the food you can eat!" And with that, the giant colonel in his giant way takes one last look at the children, then trots his horse toward the gate.

And as the soldiers stream out behind their colonel, the Dinkelsbüh-lians stream in. Look, they are hugging Lore and Elsa and Fritzie, Willie, Georgie—all the children. And they are starting to laugh and dance. The baker Mae, the tailor Tim, the Bürgermeister, even the gatekeeper, are laughing and dancing all over the square.

Later, walking home, Lore's papa strokes Lore's hair. He keeps a very straight face. "Then, Lore," he says, pulling on his chin, "there are times when children should be seen <u>and</u> heard." And he starts to say more. But look, Lore is already gone again. She is running toward her door. There is someone in her basket she wants to see.

Author's Note

This story is based on a legend still celebrated every year across the ocean in the medieval town of Dinkelsbühl, West Germany. We are not sure if Lore had a cat, or what it was that gave her enough courage to face the Swedish colonel who invaded her town. But it could have happened just like this.